San Antonio Review

The poems in this book are a compilation of carefully screened submissions to the Open City 360 Poets and Writers Group and Poets without Borders Publishing.

For information contact: director@poetswb.org or editor@poetswb.org
Cover Art © 2012 donated by Hector Lopez
Book design: Hector Lopez
Printed in the USA

First Edition

Library of Congress Cataloguing-in-Publication Data has been applied for.

The San Antonio Review Volume 1
Publishing Editor Hector Lopez
Assistant Editor Rod C. Stryker

ISBN 9780615704029

Spanish translations by Nora Gonzales
Romanian translations by Ana Nita

Publication date – August 2012

Manufactured on the third planet from the sun
@N 29° 32' 52.8256"/W 98° 17' 28.0446"

Published by Poets without Borders Small Press
146 Andorra Drive
Universal City, Texas 78148

Publicity: businessrelations@poetswb.org
Fundraising: fundraising@poetswb.org

Dedication to Hollis Walters

This inaugural printing of the San Antonio Review is dedicated to Hollis Walters, a vibrant man of eighty-three years. For years he had a well-kept secret life as a poet. Today, he is the oldest living Sun Poet and he continues to practice his passion for the art of poetry.

Born in the countryside outskirts of Livingston, Texas, Hollis graduated high school at the age of fifteen and earned a B.S. in mathematics and chemistry. At the age of twenty and with a new bride, he began his career in banking, starting out as a clerk, the lowest rung of the industry's ladder. Over fifty years later, he retired as an executive vice president of one of Houston's leading banks. The bulk of those years held Hollis's poetry in the same way a poor farmer holds the precious seeds of his crop. Poetry was and is Hollis's spiritual livelihood. He speaks of his life's lessons, of his love and joy, of his trials and tribulations through the visceral essence of his poems. He is an imagist at heart without realizing it. His style takes on a traditionalist's form, employing clear, precise images of common everyday subjects that appeal to both the casual reader and the critical one alike.

The body of work produced by Hollis includes over seven hundred poems, spanning thirty-five years. This secret endeavor, a hobby, was exposed to his colleagues when the editor of his bank's newsletter started publishing some of these poems in the late 1990's. This small effort eventually led to Hollis's poetry being included in the pages of national banking magazines. As a devoted father and husband, Hollis never let on to his family about this secret passion until after he retired. His wife knew only of the love poems he gave her on birthdays and anniversaries.

Despite the health issues that occur with the advancement of age, as well as the loss of a beloved wife, he still continues to produce this beautiful art form. It is this passion, this art of his heart that is his legacy.

Forward by Hector Lopez

The idea for this journal came to me in March of 2012. I sat in a Barnes and Noble store listening to a Sun Poets open mic session. A young woman was reciting and as her beautiful words slowly uncoiled, I fell in love with her poetry. Several excellent poets read their work that night and I found that none of them had been published. Many of these people were much like me. They wrote from their hearts, wearing their most precious and fragile organ on their sleeves. The soul displayed on stage that evening was breathtaking and worthy of recognition.

That night I slept on the idea of publishing the unknown poet, the unrecognized writer that struggles with life and all that it implies, frantically writing his thoughts in a dank poorly lit room as biting flies encircle him. I dreamed of finding the next Ai, Bukowski, Baraka, or Plath but when I awakened and drank my morning coffee, my mind settled on finding the best I could afford to publish.

Within days I had developed a plan and as I spoke to others about this, then risky venture, they looked at me with that familiar expression, "Is he crazy? Does he have any idea how much time and effort it takes to publish one journal let alone a biannual publication and anthology?" Of course, their attitudes did not faze me, I was determined.

Realizing that I had to produce a source of wealth in poetry and bring forth a product, I set out to develop a rather large online poetry workshop. I called it Open City 360 on facebook and also established a blog by the same name that contained the poetry of some of our best poets. That convinced others to come along for the ride.

The members of the Open City 360 poets group are a unique international mix of individuals from more than 25 countries that contribute to everything we have envisioned. When our membership reached 300 poets I approached the 4 individuals that I knew would prove crucial to the development of a nonprofit. Those individuals were Rod Stryker, Charles Darnell, Jennifer Yanez-Alaniz, and Akeith Walters. Collectively they form the board of directors for Poets without Borders. Without their contributions, the San Antonio Review literary journal would not exist. In addition to these individuals I would be remiss to not mention the many administrators and translators that keep both the Open City 360 workshop and blog a viable part of our project. I tip my hat and offer my heart to each of these individuals. They keep our forum clear of advertisements and links from self-serving individuals. And they also serve as catalysts by ensuring that everyone receives commentary and critique, in turn producing better poetry.

Many of the poems in this first volume are translations from their original languages. I hope that you enjoy reading the beautiful, inviting, raw, refined, and powerful poetry contained herein. With that I leave you with a quote from a man that I believe understood power and how to wield it honestly, a man that understood his own limitations.

"When power leads man toward arrogance, poetry reminds him of his limitations. When power narrows the area of man's concern, poetry reminds him of the richness and diversity of existence. When power corrupts, poetry cleanses." JFK

Introduction by Rod C. Stryker

When Hector Lopez asked me to help with editing this Journal, I was at first a little trepidacious. I know what goes into creating a literary magazine. It is at times an effort of the heart. At other times it's a joyful undertaking that can become a maddening experience.

What I found different about this Journal was the truly international effort of purely and simply telling our shared stories. In here is an exquisite collection of writers from literally around the world. You'll find so much rich texture from many different cultures as well as so much shared humanity. It has filled me with great hope and promise that we, collectively, can and must overcome all of life's challenges. And I think in these recent years, a journal like this provides a necessary panacea to the ills we keep finding ourselves entangled.

Over the past thirty years, I have been a poet, editor, and publisher. I've been blessed with meeting so many people, enjoying so many cultures, growing from so many ways of thought and self-expression. It has led me to love and pain, joy and sadness, anger and happiness, loss and reward. One thing that has eluded me was faith. In some circles, religion and/or spirituality come easily. Not so with me. I felt nothing really called to me or shook my very core. Ironically, the truth has a habit of staring you dead in the face. And fortunately, I finally woke up to my faith. Poetry: I rise from bed with my muse whispering in my ear, fall asleep to her gentle songs of love, hope and truth; dream in Elysian Fields as she gathers her sisters to dance around me in circles and light. I can never give enough of myself to the muse, but it doesn't stop me from trying, from writing as if I could.

As you read the written work in this book, I am sure you will develop a sense, as I have, that these poets understand what it means to be a writer, a poet. They too have discovered and experienced what William Carlos Williams meant when he wrote, "Poets are damned...but see with the eyes of angels." Perhaps this is dangerous thinking. Alas, we have come to such extremes in today's society. Artists and writers are shunned, ridiculed, thought less than. Equally criminal, we have accepted these notions. We've allowed those who fear new ideas, new ways of thinking to not only define us, but to also limit and/or destroy our creativity. We have developed colonized minds. But thanks to a renaissance in the creative class, publications like the San Antonio Review, and organizations like Poets without Borders, we can break those chains that have imprisoned our collective wills. We can explore where our creativity takes us, free and unfettered.

I ask everyone to join me in celebrating how each writer here embraces our very human condition. Because think about it: the force of will to possess such feelings, ideas, and ways of thinking, but also the passion to write it down AND bravely share what's been written with others is truly phenomenal. And don't just read through it in one sitting. Come back to it again and again. Dog-ear the pages of your favorite writers. Write to them. Let them know how their work has affected you. Perhaps allow yourself to finally decolonize your mind with these poems and stories. Put pen to paper. Be courageous and share with the page or with a friend your thoughts, feelings, and ideas. Share your humanity. Pay it forward. Not just for yourself, but for the world.

Who's with me?

Aleksandra Spaseska

The Other Woman

show me
how to weave
joys with unease
in morning colors
and children's eyes
with no tears shed

show me
how to unrip
this toil from my throat
clinched
by thy steps
when leaving

tell me
how to unbraid
clouds that laugh
over our street
in November.

tell me
how do you wear
that shawl of sighs
twined between
her kisses
and mine.

Sailor

I met you once, in magic days,
and marveled at the way you rolled
and how your cigarettes stayed tight,
your whiskey breath, your laughter soft
in the crosshairs of your cleft –
how you brought on board
every little newspaper and shard.

When your ship arrived, I found
Provence and the map-like furl
of each flag you chose to run.
Every little rabbit in your smile
touched me with its hops

and I wandered through the portal,
glanced one last time at your bow
tied to rocks along the shore
in a way it could not help.

You'd moved your lips and sighed
as if you needed to, and drank
looking toward, away from me
bland to the crevices of your harvest
bound up with lavender and sage.

You went to your ship,
mind filled with water's colors.

I saw a crow on the power line
replace your meadowlarks in trees,
its white splats falling under
like cloth-wrapped shrouds from June.

Pants on Fire

bad times stalk like bare-ribbed wolves
and the trees sway naked during the coldest of 'em
it doesn't make much sense
soldiers fight to save their dicks
and balls
from patient landmines
no one ever seems to talk about that
people act more like t.v. scripts
throwing faded roses at the ones biting bullets
with brittle teeth
we are told that this is patriotism
while the downward drafts
stink of bullshit
black flags unfurl across the vacancies in dirty winds…
and now
safety and decency
are just words that mean nothing
they install mirrors in coffins to open up the space
who would know, really?
being the shadow
instead of the sun
ain't so bad when you think about it

Feng Shui

Feng Shui classroom
31 teen souls
fits and misfits
pulsing, seething mass
crowded into a 625 feet square Social Studies Class

There aren't enough corners to go around!
rows nice and neat
isles full of backpacks and big awkward teen feet

Hormones, hard-ons, cleavage and thigh
at least 10 are high
and 2or 3 are struggling just to get by

A thug, a thief, a liar, a cheat
all wiggling in their seat
all seeking acceptance
all dreading exposure,
all fearing defeat

Separate as best as can be done
for they touch, twitch, and poke

They incite and entice
like hatchlings harping for food
open-beak screaming..
Me! Me! Look at me!
Some louder than others..

You, sit right over there..
last year I had your older brother!
I still have a copy of that nasty e-mail from your dysfunctional mother!

The madness abounds
it surrounds everything in the mix
I need a feng shui fix!

You, Sissy, give me that cell phone

and go wait for me in the hall…

You Three Musketeers
…all for one and one for all…
from now on each has a corner
…and keep your eyes on the wall!

You, Miss Prissy
Fixing finder nails and hair,
this is US History
….no excuses…I don't care!

There's the couple, truly in teen love
…all passion and lust

The geeks, the loner, the stoner
the over-achiever
the smart-ass who always questions the teacher
the complainers and moaners
there's 6 kids who try
…seat them center, near the front
the 10 or so semi-sane remaining serve
as a buffer between the lower 50% Bell Curve.

In this confining square box are files, computers, and such
Is there some space for a teacher?
Is that asking too much?
Books and backpacks, bulletin boards
All in disarray
….There's got to be a feng shui way!

Desks, tables, piles and piles of papers
saved projects all crowded in this tiny space
I need someone to clean up the places!
Where to put these people?
Where to put the stuff?

What the heck, it's September,
June will come soon enough!

David McLean

The Winter Wakens

the winter wakens in us
skilled and proficient at being
like Didier Drogba running
just because he can, and the ball at his feet
is snow and life sleeping
under the tired skin of mud and ice

and there are no goals and goalposts
just being alive and not worrying
about entropy and time
like Nietzsche with a broken umbrella
he has never forgotten anywhere
yet, we are alive again and consent

David McLean

Centers

so here are centers and the decentralized,
a sullen technical necessity
and fragments of sex and bodies gone
like Spinoza in a nightgown
hunting Guattari with a gun

because jealousy is the supple motion
of subtle numbers
it is chasing verification
like all the sentences poets have written
without any clear meaning,

or like Spinoza in a nightgown,
like Guatarri sleeping

The Tunnel

the tunnel is gray
with sea at the end of it
and the vampires stagger
because it is the 1960s
and Jean Rollin is after them
with a homoerotic vengeance

words like stones under water
each torn to a splendid isolation
refusing to assemble into dialog
because there is no dialog
or incontrovertible converse
anywhere

except in tunnels through love
and excavations under childhoods
that probably never happened

and living a life
was raping a vampire
because time is blind
because the castle is a shabby farmhouse
with answers in it

it is emptiness
and the insolence of things
it is a pointless idol
a piano probably
but nobody sings

Yair Ben-Zvi

It's the Everyday Thief

It's the everyday that's the thief; it's the everyday that kills

He and I had walked the hill and remained standing despite the strains in our legs and pains in our bodies.

We saw cities and people the one a chamber of echoes the other screaming to be heard.

We breathed deep and looked up. He talked to me, I ignored him. He talked again and tried an accent, asked if that was better, I was shamed enough to laugh.

The sun was just beginning to set. We had come to talk of thoughts and dreams and projects and goals. What to write, what to try, what to put down, what to to try again, and what it is we wanted to do.

But the sun kept going down and what came was thus: Jobs, bosses, errands, families, bills, favors, friends, climbing the ladder and falling into poverty, gotta eat to live and live to eat, need that wall with a door, need this need that, need it now, need it yesterday, do this when, do this now, our lives may have belonged to us at some point, but our time was a loan, we had the moments between promises, obligations, and debts. Be thankful, it has been said, or please be quiet.

We separated down the hill and he promised me I'd see him again, saying he had to sleep for tomorrow he worked. I did too.

I couldn't then, and cannot now still, stop thinking, about this one little fundamentalism: the brighter the light, the longer the shadow.

Dove Holes

See the sky-barn door swing
back and forth, but never close,
while the wild flowers dip their heads
avoiding not succumbing.
Not yet.

------- o -----------------------

In chosen pockets of calm and shelter
of shadow and moss
you do the same
and he watches you.
He says nothing
and he lacks nothing.

---------------- o -------------

Later the train stops, suddenly.
The unexpected East End
falls into your lap
excuses himself and looks away.

--------------------- o -------

You feel his hands on your thighs still
strong hands, hands that could hurt,
or pick you up with ease.
And you have not yet
passed Dove Holes,
where any man can be king
for a day.

--------------------------------O.

Fallen

She'd had a rye life,
whisky eyes
seen through ice cube charms,
propped up on a bar stool pedestal
accepting only liquid worship -

no chasers for her,

and I caught her eye
as she swept the bump 'n' grind persona
of Friday night whores,
draped Dali like across wide-boys arms.

Her half moon smile
tainted by nicotine clouds
as they fought to escape
the confines of an inhale,
and me the rabbit in headlights glare,
tongue tied to this table,
nursing a misplaced conception.

She was slick as she oozed
through the waves of melded bodies,
caught in a chimera of sex and music;
a deep throb within.

Another notch to be nicked
in her playground stick,
a passing phase
in her latest craze,

she was warm in my lap
like a pile of bones before the pyre,
waiting .. just waiting,

and I found I could climb
the ladder of her spine, though her heart
had escaped that cage long ago,

all I could see was my dignity
lying discarded on an unmade bed,

and her proclaiming
"I used to be a lady."

Poise

your body in the depth of my hands
muscles like lazy snakes
under high-noon sun
on smooth, time-burnished stone
Laocoon's forbidden pleasure
redeemed
by benevolent gods' absolution

yet the fibre is tense
strained by unseen chords
like an instrument tuned to play
or a cave man ready to hunt

I try to eternise you in this poise
to imprint the seal of your limbs
on the vellum of my skin
but my colours blur
and I sense a trace of dust
in the depth of my palms

The Last Refugee

I

And here We stand
on the edge of Man's eye,
weathered shoulders upon wearier shoulders,
the last of Us,
remnants of a cold decaying Truth.

II

Where art thou, Brother?
Quo vadis, Brother?
left me shattered, spited, sprained,
torn apart from mother's dew
silenced was my father's tongue.
and here I stand Now, unbound.

III

The indignant centuries
weather us down
to here, where We
can bare no more...
no soothing cascades of respite,
no damn salvation in sight...
Hope's residue, an elapsed relic,
a remnant of what was once
but no longer due.
I follow you into the mirage...
I
follow
you.

IV

Laid upon a maiden's breasts
once I caressed a dream so young,
eyes scattered to a world so new.

Now ireful, intact, immured
I lay my wretched body to rest.
I call thee, Brother, come,
lay my body to rest.

V

It falls unto whom at best
I besiege to learn...
to form Truth into a surrogate pillow
from the cadaver of a dying
crest fallen star?

We have lived and have laid together,
blanketed by the same silver thorns of night
adorning the same shy veil,
we have danced together through images
of a million such fire borne and bred tales...
and yet we remain so few,
amidst so many...
the last stuttering embers
of Humanity's flame.

VI

I will turn to Sun and Moon
I shall prevail the scorn and yearn
I will walk the tall and deep
echoes of serenity.

Reborn, these eyes will see
through the wilderness of
life retold in
bearing mothers
weeping children
fallen heroes
of embodied Times to be.
I shall be free, my Brother
in the echo of your Soul.

VII.1

Hush now child of etched dreams,
it seems you are the brother
to the children of the world,
have no doubt.

Destiny painted across the palettes of
night and dark,
a forgiven Hope
yet to spark
within the mist laid
enclaves
of a forgotten tombstones'
serenade.
Hush...
the world we seek
is yet to come.

VII.2

No matter
how wondrous or venomous
that world might be,
How older or colder
I may grow,
I shall be embraced
in its motherly love,
ever so thrilling.
East and West
colliding on my restless wings,
Head sprouting
on the mounting North
Abundant dreams
weaving in the plenteous South.
There I shall lay my bones
unchained, unbroken, undenied
Eyes persevering
the humbleness of time
Hands locked
in perpetual prayer,
and oh, what a lulling

mausoleum that would be
for my invictus soul.

Lawn Furniture

A year after we moved
Monte put the couch out,
a brick under one corner to level
—for curb appeal

the old place was cheap rent,
a 10-year fixer-upper with
a third entry sided over on the outside
doorknob to nowhere still intact inside

and this was the wider way in for
the brown tweed, trendy for its time;
made amputee on the way out

the couch sat on the lawn
for less than an hour when
someone rang the bell, drove away happy,
the brick thrown into the bargain

and when I heard about
what happened . . . I wondered how long
the couch balanced on that brick, or was still,
because people rarely off themselves
sitting on brown tweed.

Perigee Pearl

The moon was full of spoon-fed pearls looped
'round wedding day necks; and Steinbeck knew
of black and white and no in-between nooses.

Shakespeare coveted his. Keats wondered
at heroism. Banality claiming this moon doesn't
look much bigger than yesterday's retreats to
her trough. And

but for the mosquito who sampled the free wine bar,
I might have lingered to pay further homage with
an attentive thought.

In 1980, for ten dollars a woman dived for oyster;
a pearl plucked from its gelled host appraised
at ten dollars.

These Provisions

I must tunnel to Hell first through your
barricaded heart. The night watchman
says he hears you curse my name : the
silence of time, yes, I admit, can be as
deafening as all that too, but I tell him
nothing more. We've outlasted all the
gimcrackery and avoidance together.

-

Onto the shelf I watch you put the regular
junk of an everyday life : cornflakes and
maple syrup, tomato sauce and a jar of
pickled beets. No matter; these things
just are, like the smile on your face.

-

Somewhere behind my head, your
stupid music goes on : boys singing
about girls or girls singing about boys.
It's everywhere the same - the loveless
seeking love, or those in passion seeking
an out. Sex and madrigals, organ
preludes, all that a'capella crap.

-

I no longer have the hesitation needed
to run after yet another dream. It was
once a dream of you, but I've placed
that too on the shelf we've stacked.

My Lasting Aversion to Light Years and Lust

The man's scrawly hand left a message on
the window grime - 'I would want to either
discuss this or kill you.' A Hallmark Card
only by degrees. He called himself Zou-Zou
and went to great ends to make it work.
'I have a lasting aversion to light years
and to lust, just the same and together
separate. Doesn't matter. When I wing a
turkey, that turkey stays winged.'
-

How can one deal with this stuff? If I was
a Detective Bob Eddy or someone like that,
I'd suppose I could just take him down; telling
him, 'your on my case-load now buddy, and this
is taken as a threat and I'm bringing you in.'
Would that work, I wonder? As it is, I am a
layman with but a skillful aversion to early
death or to being wounded in the foul pursuit
of someone else's homicidal goals. 'I'll sign
whatever you wish, just get this bastard gone.'
-

That was all imagined; it never worked out that way.
He was my friend when we were nine. I remember him
at sixteen, getting his first taste of a girl and trying to
tell me about it. Then, at twenty-three, he was in
Vietnam, 'lifting a leg,' he said, 'to piss on a gook'.
Then, no contact for over thirty years. And now this -
he's in that dead-man box in the funeral home,
out there somewhere too, with his stick, poking
his holes in the cosmos, I guess.

Mexican Zombism Haiku

Mexican Zombism: Haiku No. 1

Mama-Lia's Menudo:
the official sponsor of
the Apocalypse

Mexican Zombism: Haiku No. 2

Chola was chula
until her inner zombie
bit into my skin

Mexican Zombism: Haiku No. 3

"Run for the border!"
and scream like hell to warn us
zombie fiesta

Mexican Zombism: Haiku No. 4

Mexican zombies:
because living death never
smelled so damned spicy

Mexican Zombism: Haiku No. 5

And then it happen
Night of the Walking Cholos
bad batch of nachos

Tristesse of Excess

1.

I used to lose myself in the depths of her flesh
plumbing for that one true light.
She once was a sustainable source.
Now she hisses if I remove my clothes.
We merge for a distant minute then she disconnects, turns away,
faces a solitary crack in the wall – dry as her own.
I dangle myself from the side of the bed; test the weak light with my toes –
a child left alone by the side of a pool, traitor cold.
On this precipice I weave my shadow.
I read her some Plato, it puts her to sleep. I arrive dead in her dreams.
Exposed, I wrap her body in an indigo sheet.
Beyond the open window, the wheat seethes, the crows sing murder ballads.
I send them my mind, hoping they can find the kill switch.

2.

I was once his flower, his flame, the light bouncing across his eyes.
Now he is just a clumsy hunter that cravenly shoots his game from behind.
Disfiguring the grace of my body's generosity; barely hard enough to even
enter me. Over in a tepid thirty seconds. He can't look me in the eye. I roll
away.
He gets up, runs water, I think of the brown horses and burnished hills of my
youth.
The shadows play soft upon my skin.
He returns, reads Plato aloud, bereft of passion.
His hands, his tongue – careless knives, cold and stained.
Coward of the light. Cowan of the darkness. He shivers in between,
clothed only in his guilt. If he would just shut up;
defenestrate himself from the window I left open for him –
the birds would sing satin lullabies, I'd sleep soundly,
silhouetted in the light he missed.

Just a Shadow

After birth altricial,
flight is tested.

She lifts her veil –
an apocalypse
honest blue and beautiful.

Pale bouquet becomes this
Ophelia rising from her stream.

A bright dream wrecked
by morning's darkness.

The feeding hand
she says tastes like ashes
is wholly her own.

The horses are hard rain in the stable.
She fixes a bath.

Another wobbling planet
mirrored in the water.
From a distance gentled.
Still close up the naked eye finds hunger –
a blind familiar savage, coldly encroaching.

She knows of a clearing where
the dog's tracks merge with those of the hunted –
just a flash, a flame of late sun on fading snow.
The arrow's immediacy is finally softened there.

She lays herself down in that minor place
beyond the blood dappled brambles,
safely finds herself a cord of wood –
a fire that burns itself alive to live.

The world is ending
in a way too human to believe.

Sudden night comes as burial above ground.
She closes her eyes to see.

The light aches to speak
in shadows long and lean
a language profoundly meaningless –
now the breath is gone.

The Passion of Ferdinand

Make way for Ferdinand,
who refused his horns their use,
twin spears, twin spires uplifted
in offering to the lords of pollen
to the goddesses of bloom--
wreath them in hyacinths, these horns,

bring bouquets to line the path for his delicate hooves,
cloven, cleaving to the patient earth
and like Io I'll low and loll in his fields.

This prince of peace whose beautiful resistance
stayed the sword, who sat and inhaled
the perfumed taboo, great haunches bundled,
power arrested in the sand--

will there be ever be another bull like him?
Let him reign under his cork-tree,
beast of great blossoming, whose life
forgives, forgives the boys
who shove who punch who rut
in the burgeoning pasture below
where I await his blessing.

Colin Dardis

Euphoria

It is dawn and I have awoken
to the grey becoming bronze,
familiar wash of spring blue
soaks the rolling eye of earth,
nature blinks another day
out into the horizons.

The simple delight of catching daybreak
climb over the dampened rooftops,
mildew slates glisten with all the elegance
of functional architecture.

There is no dawn chorus
in the big city.

Our nests filled with the cavalcade
of motor car and pedestrian talk,
morning chatter of daily commutes
filled with echoes of the previous night
and the splutters of shift workers
tying up their starts and ends;
an ever reliant engine ignites
and the grim driver curses its obedience.

The sustenance of hot water
collapses into sinks, showers and coffee mugs
while millions contemplate retirement
over their bowel-conscious cereals,
and I lie on in bed,
waiting for the cattle roar
to drive the herd forward.

I Will Speak More and More Softly

I will speak more and more softly
until my words are whispered
like those of sinner
in the confessional

I will whisper more and more softly
until I susurrate
like leaves
in the wind

I will susurrate more and more softly
until my voice resembles
the voice of the sand
by the sea

Night 1088

The night is a rare steak poked with a fork.
If it could bleed on us, it would. The ground
is tender and shiny, wet and warm. It gulps
at the very bottoms of our feet, sucks softly
at the skin. The moon is high, the moon is
super, the moon is our only witness. You
walk ahead of me. Your shoulders are down,
your pageboy cap is leaving a familiar mark
on the brick wall beside us. I know that shadow.
I am the one who has seen it the most. I can
tell from its slump and lean that something
isn't quite right tonight. I do not ask what it is,
but instead, focus on the smoosh of our feet
being taken in by the soft ground. I focus on
the one little raindrop sliding down my nose.

Technicolor Rainbow Emotions

I dream in Technicolor rainbow emotions
I live in the mansion of my empathy
Every room I make
holds my sanguine disposition
the blue room, calm and quiet
the black room, where my anger is kept
in a little music box on the mantel
the red room throws caution to the wind and
colors carelessly whisper
forgotten passions and carnal pleasure
The green room holds fairy dust in a forest of
whimsy and delight
my nectar is held under leaves surging from beautiful branches
My Technicolor life leads me to peace.

Zachary Guadamour

Dawn

We dress slowly
conscious of common property
an extension of our loving
cultivation of a new tropical flower
the private country in which we wander

We skirt the silken mounds of a dune
come to a bare plateau
surface worn smooth by centuries of blowing sand
even the colored striations honed and fine to the touch
nails worked by an emery board and held up to the light

I forget the insects in our lives
smothered in copper coils and false pearls
crawling over memory and buzzing into our past
flying off into whatever future we share

The Loneliness and a Bed

right after we fucked
she lit two cigarettes
in the darkness of her lips
& handed me one

"seeing the
world for what it is
really hurts," she said

i said nothing
letting the tip of my
cigarette
become the light for
the both of us

i was just too
tired to
die.

Forgotten Lives

Their bones dance in the wind,
skulls rolling haltingly in the dust
to rest a kilometer away in dry river beds,
amidst piles of rot and souls in commune,
that hug and hide their faces
from the disdain of the land that bore them.
The black feathery beasts of the wild
circle, as if haunted, and map the expanse
for the freshness of death.
They watch bemused at the hopelessness
of children crawling on their bellies defeated,
and parents blankly stare – tears.

The old, having witnessed life in passing
wait patiently for their souls to desert them.
Their bodies are ant hills of jutting bones
their lips dry, cracking, and pursed –
their tongues have lost ownership of words.
There is no need to speak; no sounds come out
of a belly sunk and plastered on bent spine.
The lungs can no longer hold air for a full breath;
gasps and little coughs squeeze
out of a throat taunting – to close.

Where are the city folks with glistening skins,
cultured accents, and famine solutions to boot?
Do they think of the child that crawls to death
a few hours away, under the roasting sun?
Where are the ministers, with broad grins
and a wealth of verbiage to shoot?
Did they not make the garbage collector
and gas stations wealthy men?
Yet behind their mansions, the young
cuddle garbage cans for warmth;
their mouths frothy with refuse and gum.
Voiceless, their only distress call is a sigh,
before they pass away – waiting for us.

Abandoned in misery's dark corners, children
wasting; their shriveled behinds gashed with deep lines,
their bones covered by dried-out skin,
pause for us to temper the vagaries of nature
and trap the vestiges of our selfishness.
We walk on – without a care!
But the face of a suffering child is the heart of God
reaching out to stir the depths of our being.
Let's desire nothing, than to see others too
experience relief and joy.

***

Vultures watch the tussle between soul and body,
celebrate as the body tumbles and stills in the hazy heat,
and moves in – to have a fill.

Charlie Vazquez

"The Man Who Kept Walking"

Inspired by the film "El Color de la Guayaba"
directed by Luis Caballero...

As sunset's shadow slipped down the mountain
Caressing the jungles ripe with guayaba trees
The man who kept walking awoke and slipped
His favorite shoes onto his tired timeless feet

Following the quick retreat of light to darkness
He started at the starkness of the plaza where
People, not noticing him, turned in for the night
Although his holy work was just about to begin

Leaving the tiny pueblo and passing grand fincas
He didn't take notice of churches and schools
Trappings of mortals, but walked a straight line
To the beach, until the green sea rose over his head

And kept walking.

During the Days with Little Sun

It is already winter.
I sneak images into my sight.
I hollow the black and white photographic corpse and I reach out with my hands.

To enfold is a sort of a defense. An askew lack of prop when to have is the same as to be. Actually you didn't exist for the old tongues. The same way I shall have not been at a late time and I doubt of us ever meeting again. There are neither other shores, either another dimension, nothing would ever tell us to make everything right if we were to be others, meeker. I hallowed the cross made of tiles mother was fretting the incense the candles the wheat porridge the priest the crosses the wine yes father, maybe now he will stay still to rest his silence given by you.

We function; hanged by deadlines and paid bills the tally of all celebrations or other lonely notes.

Kenneth Slaathaug

Slang

standing on a rock
with a wind-eroded torso,

a mushroom cloud frozen
in time but teetering on a
precipice,

awaiting the right moment
in the future to become
another member of the
Boot Hill gang,

the land will remain
as the buttes erode
themselves first into
faux mushroom clouds
and then into shattered
elegance,

and then and only then
will the slang become
null and void

X & Y

X said to Y,
I got a job today.

Y said to X,
What do you do now?

X said,
I mark spots.

Y said,
Why is that?

X said,
Because you always ask
the most important questions.

Y blushed,
That's true.

X stated,
I need a partner though,
because this new job
requires two-man teams.

Y answered,
I'd be glad to help
but I get paid rather
handsomely for what
I do now.

X added,
The pay is easily
three times more
than what you are
getting now.
That was all Y needed to here
and she reported to Descartes
Industries the next day.

Ever since, X & Y fell in
love, got married
and had infinitely
many children called
ordered pairs.

As for Y's former profession,
the bosses at Philosophers Unlimited
hired a three-letter word that made
the same sound, and things have been
squarer than a circle ever since.

Even Jerusalem Artichokes

I plant a little of everything
in my garden,
beans and corn,
Argentine squash,
Chinese parsley,
Andean potatoes,
even Jerusalem artichokes.
Everything fits
and ripens
without elitism.
Some even nourish,
pollinate one another.
I just provide a little soil,
water and harvest,
everything in its own time
throughout the seasons.
There are no borders
in my garden.
Everything emigrates,
immigrates,
even Jerusalem artichokes.

SOUR

she inhaled, a sour essence of creativity she talked barefoot and teasingly
her hair like aspen exhaling her dragon high on the hill and when she did
pass it was to new heights I could not have imagined she brings my smile so
easily

lips like sugar echoed the Bunnymen in the brown station wagon of joy fire
flies flickered against the stars her hands upon the red dust of Mars she
giggled at the faintest noise

her posture and poise and of the world she told what she knew enlightened
in her truths, and the loves that she blue collected thoughts she held on to
like childhood toys

midnight daisies share her space as she ponders the sour taste

and like a dragon she said "am I poetry?" as she floated towards the fields
ready for harvest

Mi Primo Segundo (My Second Cousin)

Miguel, Mike, Miguel, who cares?
I remember him driving
a Volkswagen Beetle, delivering pizza.

Mike, 6 feet tall, like a telephone pole,
Sera retarded? A girl jested.

Some people are just not good with languages.
Miguel being one, on top of that he was a stutterer.

Can you imagine speaking Spanish with a stutter?
Think, Mel Tillis. Miguel was no singer—
so pile on that learning English.

As a kid, he easily took to pop culture, hip-hop,
skateboarding, handball.

Mike could work. When he was fifteen,
in the evenings, he washed dishes and pots
at Jay's Diner—off the books.

On weekends, he shoveled snow,
and threw out the trash, paid in cash.

After a job, he would say,
Pagame me-me lo-lo que tu-tu puedes,
pay me what you want, hoping for the best.

In school, he was in the progress class,
the one other kids ran from.

But I knew there wasn't anything wrong
with him, that a little English could not cure.

A Leaf Unseen

A leaf gets detached
From a dust-laden tree,
In a corner street full of
Egg shells and residues of
Some hotel dinner;
The yellow veined leave,
Vulnerable,
Flying in the hot air
For some distance,
Then dropping down on the
Dusty ground of the gasping city,
Covered with thick smog;
The tender leave,
Uprooted,
Settles down on the uneven street,
Slowly being trampled by the
Hurried feet, on way to offices/schools,
The trampling of the little leaf,
Unseen on this melancholy morning;
Like---
The crying of a girl-child,
Standing solitary at the locked gate,
Calling for an absent mother,
Or,
An old man trying repeatedly
The long-distance number
Of a son who never responds,
Having erased all the memories of
A loving parent and Indian childhood/youth,
In his Florida home.
The leaf that once fluttered,
Gave shade,
As part of tree green,
Has outlived its value,
For some
In the commercial city,
And---
Now,

Fallen and flattened,
Is mourned by none.

Phil Kanyonyozi

Of Shades of War and Peace

I pray for the day when I will not have to pray
For a better day, but shall watch the sun rise
On the stretched horizon in bright rose-flushes
Which outstretch bouquets of red dawns
In romantic overtures that shall rekindle
The light of peace in a world at high noon
Where war is an answer that begs the question
Whether humanity is not human but is an idea
Best expressed by how wild animals treat their own.

Or maybe Darwin was wrong and man devolved
From hominid-nude to Nuclear weaponry-rude
Awakening a martial spirit with war-like aphides
Sapping the flower of new beginnings that crept over
The Garden of Eden in emerald rugs scattered
Here and there with lilies that danced in the wind
To Nature's sweet symphony of calm and quiet.

Instead the eves of twilight have stolen the sun
And replaced it with war-darkened shorelines
Whose beachheads have pushed man to the brink
Of a conflagration that will kill man over and over
As his suicidal flesh turns to dust, blown in harsh winds
That will forever blind him to what lies ahead.

Public Auction

They trade with my dreams
training their skills
They shop with my temper
dabble their patience
They bet for my breast
Measure their libido
They drink for my health
get drunk with their money
They are sleepless
Concerned about my problems
They hire a private detective
to write my black biography
counting my lovers.
For all the time
For them
I'm at the public auction
And they try to steal my eye
To rape my dream
to push me in the hinterland
And to play, play with me.

Coffee Stains

My life has been marked by coffee stains on white shirts.
My soul is drenched in rivers of black and pools of white
Mixed in with brown sugar covered up in a layer of cream.
And I have made my life a mess by adding artificial sweeteners,
Distracting cancer-causing diversions
That take away from the experience we're really meant to taste.
I remember spilling the mocha when I heard what she said.
And now the smell of coffee beans in coffee shops is synonymous
With narrow eyes and familiar discontent.
These stains never really come out.
Not even with highly industrialized psychiatric bleach
And there's never any sense in hiding it.
Someone will always point them out.

I have fluctuated between sweet and bitter,
My words are strong and bold,
And my personality now mild.
Taste and see to know who I am;
My blood now saturated with caffeine and
My dreams now ground up into fine powder for the world's consumption.
And now I'm too afraid to wear white shirts
For fear that I will dirty them with black stains.
Once they're there, they never really go away.
My life has been measured out by coffee stains
Calling out to passer-bys, begging to be noticed,
And nothing I do between this life and the next
Could save me from the precarious trapeze act that I so awkwardly perform.
The world cheers with me when I triumph on these high wires,
But it waits and watches with anticipation for my fall.

Too afraid to see, too naive to speak
But all I have left between this life and the next
Are a motley collection of coffee stains,
Ugly and desperate testimonies that I have tried so hard to clean.
Still. Bring me the mochas of victory,
And the lattes of deep contrition.
Bring me the jovial macchiato and the courageous, bold Americano!
I will drink them all!

Because between this life and the next, I am convinced
A secret from the Kingdom of God has been passed down to me...
That somewhere between the first, steaming morning cup and the evening dose with friends,
This strung-out life is way too short to worry about coffee stains.

34

It's a restless sleep, the most dangerous thing were it to be over.
The memories are always the same dream: a repeated sea
with huge waves that move away and come back taking and bringing
garbage and pieces of heaven.
That's my recurrent life's dream.

Sometimes I forget that the night extends
beyond the roof. I forget that outside
air is being breathed and voices are being heard.
There's no less chaos, there's a different chaos.

When I finally saw her it became clear to me that she will hang on my neck
forever
as a precious necklace made of brief eternal moments. That her ephemeral
truth
will reveal the most ephemeral moment of true
happiness which I will only recognize after it has ceased.

Doors have closed, I've closed them.
I will leave behind obsolete baggage that slows me.
I feel the change, I feel like my old skin peel,
I feel brightly colored feathers and hard as scales.

The new version of me doesn't have possessions yet, nothing tangible,
everything to be cared and to be despised lies inside.
The outer cover serves only to move, it's only a suit,
a costume, a dying leaf.

My debts are paid, I declare myself free.
It's time to start collecting new ones.

Another Letter to God

We need to talk

We need to do something about our relationship
that's been a bit strained
on the outs
sailing on rough seas
these past couple of decades
We need to either come to some sort of agreement
or simply part ways

I need to know
what it is you want from me?
Because, truth be told, I'm not asking anything from you
other than to be left alone
I've heard the sermons
and the promises
of eternal salvation
everlasting peace
a place in Heaven
But I want to hear it from you
I've heard it all from the MEN here on earth
but now I want to hear it from YOU
What do you want from me?

Why do you keep testing me?
I don't do tests
and you should know this
I don't want to prove myself worthy
or earn my spot 'up there'....
I've pretty much come to live by the Blood, Sweat and Tears song
that says 'I swear there ain't no Heaven and I pray there ain't no Hell'
But yet, you continue to test me....
and I continue to fail....

Yes, I've heard the sermons
the bible-thumping
fire and brimstone
fear of God speeches

but I don't listen
because I can't understand how a father would really want his children
to fear him
rather than love him....
to have blind faith in him
rather than know him....

And this whole OCD thing?
I don't get it
I don't like it
and I don't want it
and if suffering through it
for a lifetime down here
is my ticket to eternal salvation up there
well then....
you know how I feel....

So c'mon, let's talk
I mean, really talk
no subtle signs
or hints
or hidden signposts along the way
let's just talk....

I'm willing to listen if you are....

Contributors Notes and Comments

Advait Praturi is a mix of many different things poured into one confused bundle of sinews and bones. Hip hop, faith, business, art, poetry, spoken word, economics, foreign policy and politics, and a heart for people all thrown into one. He has lived in Mumbai, India for the past 2 years. He currently works as an outreach coordinator for a foreign policy think tank there.

Aleksandra Spaseska was born in 1984 in the town of Kavadarci, Macedonia. Spent her childhood and early adolescence in her parents' hometown of Prilep where she first started writing poetry and short stories. At the age of 18 she moved to the capital Skopje where she enrolled in the Department of English language and literature at the faculty of philology. She currently works as a translator for the daily newspaper "Vest" and is also engaged as a freelance journalist for SkopjeUrbanStyle website. Her poems were included in several collaborative issues of poetry, the online student magazine "Izlez", the blog Open City 360 Poets and Writers and The Anthology of Young Macedonian Avant-garde Poetry, and she is a member of the non-profit literary arts organization Poets without Borders. She now writes both in Macedonian and English, mostly poetry.

April Michelle Bratten is a writer currently living in the sad plains of North Dakota. She has been previously published in Istanbul Literary Review, The Santa Fe Literary Review, and Gutter Eloquence Magazine, among others. Her full length collection of poetry, It Broke Anyway, will be released on NeoPoeisis Press later this year. She co-edits the online literary journal Up the Staircase Quarterly.

Dr. Aprilia Zank is a freelance lecturer in the Department of Languages and Communication at Ludwig Maximilian University of Munich, Germany, where she tutors Creative Writing Workshops. Aprilia is also a poet and a translator, as well as editor of an English - German poetry anthology. She writes verse in English and German, and was awarded a distinction at the "Vera Piller" Poetry Contest in Zurich. She is also a passionate photographer.

Charlie Vázquez is the Bronx-born author of the novels Buzz and Israel and Contraband, and the bilingual poetry collection Meditations/Meditaciones: Bronx/Salsa. He has edited and co-edited two anthologies of new Latino literature: The Best of PANIC! And From Macho to Mariposa: New Gay

Latino Fiction.

Colin Dardis born at the tail end of the seventies in Northern Ireland is a poet, artist, and performer. He edits Speech Therapy, an online zine focusing on poetry from Ireland and beyond. He is also the founder of Purely Poetry, an open mike poetry night in Belfast, and member of the performance group, Voica Versa. Colin's work has been previously in numerous anthologies, journals and zines in Ireland, the UK and the USA.

Colin Marschall lives in the United Kingdom. He is a member of various poetry groups. He takes great pleasure in writing free verse poetry.

Dan Iancu was born in Bucharest, Romania in 1956. He is a graduate of Mathematics Faculty. Dan has been writing poetry for many years and in 1998 won his first poet contest from "Cartea Romaneasca" publishing house with "About Meaning", his first poetry collection. Afterwards he published "Boston my Love", "A Rock Saying", "The Father Only Photos", and "We, a Half God".

Dario R. Beniquez is the founder and facilitator of the Gemini Ink Open Writers Workshop, San Antonio, Texas. He has been published in *Voices de la Luna, Rio Grande Review, Texas Observer,* and *Chrysalis.*

David McLean has lived in Sweden since 1987. He lives there on a small island in the Mälaren with partner, weather, boat, dog and cats. In addition to six chapbooks, McLean is the author of three full-length poetry collections: CADAVER'S DANCE (Whistling Shade Press, 2008), PUSHING LEMMINGS (Erbacce Press, 2009), and LAUGHING AT FUNERALS (Epic Rites Press, 2010).

Eric Biggs is a retired attorney from Santa Fe, NM. He resides in the Philippines where he has established a new life with a new wife. His residency there has continued to inspire his writings, especially in his continuing pursuit to establish a more perfect poetic form.

Frank Reardon was born in Boston, Massachusetts but has lived all over the world. His first book, Interstate Chokehold, was released via Neo Poiesis Press in 2009. His second book, The Nirvana Haymaker, also from Neo Poiesis Press, is due out this fall. He's currently working on a 3rd collection for Punk Hostage Press and a Novel. Frank has been published in various print & online magazines.

Gary Introne is a writer and artist residing in Metuchen, NJ, who spends his time between NYC, Princeton University (where he works in the University Bookstore), and Philadelphia, PA. His works include 'Rome's Roads', 'Riding the Descant', 'Life Wars', and 'the Miasma Arms Hotel'. In addition, 20 of his paintings have recently sold to a collector in Beijing, China, and are represented in various other USA locations.

Ilire Zajmi lives in the Republic of Kosovo. Ilire is the author of seven books that include 3 collections of poetry. Her books have been published in a variety of languages which include Albanian, Portuguese, Italian, and English.

Jabez W. Churchill was born in Northern California, educated in Argentina, California, and Cuba. He is a single father, currently teaching modern languages at Santa Rosa Junior College and Mendocino College, and has been a California Poet in the Public Schools since 1998. He has practiced civil disobedience since 1970, and submitted poetry for publication since 1979. He is widely published.

Jay Halsey "When Jay Halsey isn't too strung out from the work week grind helping feed folks unluckier than himself along the Colorado front range, he spends time with his wife, reads many books, writes poetry, stomps around old, dusty places to shoot photos, drinks beer and whiskey, and talks to the neighborhood cats Of course, not necessarily in that order."

Juan Manuel Perez is a Mexican-American poet. He is the author of Another Menudo Sunday (2007), O' Dark Heaven: A Response to Suzette Haden Elgin's Definition of Horror (2009), WUI: Written Under the Influence of Trinidad Sanchez, Jr. (2011), and six poetry chapbooks. Juan is also the 2011-2012 Poet Laureate for the San Antonio Poets' Association, not to mention, the best known Chupacabra Poet on this planet.

Kenneth Slaathaug is an aspiring poet who combines a deep well of useless knowledge and mathematical insight into something that might read well only once. He has a strong love for the downtrodden and the family life. He is happily married and has a beautiful daughter. He currently resides in Bismarck, North Dakota.

Pablo Hernández M. was born in Guatemala City, Guatemala. Has been writing regularly since 2003 in different blogs presently in 'La voz dentro'. In 2011, his book 'En lo invisible' was published in blog format and it can be read for free. Pablo is a business administrator that enjoys reading, writing, and growing orchids.

Philip Matogo, was born April 2, 1974, in Uganda. He was schooled in various countries. He earned a degree in Mass Communication at Makerere University, Kampala. He has published one prose book, "Fabric of Grey". He has another prose book, "Whispers in the Sky" and a poetry anthology, "Nocturnes at Dawn" on the horizon. He works for the Ugandan Ministry of Defense.

Priyanka Dey is a poet and blogger and is currently the Managing Editor of Verse and Verse Magazine in India. She is currently working on a poetry anthology.

Rene Velez was born and raised in New York City. He has great insight into the human condition and this is reflected in his verse. He has been writing poetry for fifteen years.

Richard M. Oduor Richie Macs (alias Richie Maccs) is a son of Africa, 28 years old, and a citizen of Kenya. He lives and works in Nairobi. He writes poems courageous enough to break the walls of silence, to inspire meditations on life and connect souls with pure essences. His words clean and remold the bedraggled scarecrow that our world has become. They dance each morning on paper and invite you to look deeper – to share your heart-prints.

Syed Shehzar Mukkarrim Doja born in Dhaka, Bangladesh, is a student of English Literature, Psychology, and Philosophy at Fergusson College in Pune, India. Doja loves poetry and looks forward to becoming a full-time writer.

Steve Johnson a.k.a. Dr. Waldazo is a San Antonio resident for the past 25 years. He draws inspiration for his poetry from a career in public education, his early childhood living in foreign countries, his family life, and his love of motorcycling.

Sunil Sharma, India-born, suburban Mumbai-based, is a college principal, a prolific literary-fiction writer, poet, freelance journalist, critic, reviewer, interviewer and editor. He is widely published, both on-line and in the print literary journals of international repute. Many of his shorts and poems have been anthologized internationally. He is on the edit board of many journals as adviser. So far, Sunil has published a novel, a collection of poems, edited jointly a book of stories and about to publish more in near future.

Thomas D. Jones has two books of poetry published--Voices from the Void, 2008 and Genealogy X, 2001--plus publications in anthologies, literary magazines, blogs, and websites throughout the country. He holds a BA and MA and teaches English as a Second Language and remedial reading and writing.

Tia Downe (Tiana Bezmenova) was born and raised in California and now resides in San Antonio TX. She has been writing poetry for more than a decade. She is an art and music lover and surrounds herself with art whenever possible. She finds inspiration in the writers Poe, Shakespeare, Dickinson and Frost.

Tria Wood was born in San Antonio, and resides Houston, Texas, where she teaches creative writing at San Jacinto College. Her poetry, fiction, and reviews have appeared in *Snowy Egret*, *Concho River Review*, *Arcadia*, and other publications. Along with sculptor Tara Conley She created "My Life as a Doll," a large-scale literary art installation. It was exhibited at Diverse Works Arts-pace in Houston in the fall of 2011.

Vincent Aurelius lives in Paris, France. He is a British writer and a member of the London-based Fledgling Arts Collective which champions all forms of art while helping especially those with mental health and other problems. His poems and short stories have been published on three continents. He often writes very quickly and edits his own work at glacial pace, the result being a rich mixture of instinct and craft. His work is also coloured by earlier incarnations as a stand-up-comic, university lecturer and psychiatric nurse.

Wanda Morrow Clevenger lives in Hettick, IL. Over 150 pieces of her work appear in 58 print and electronic publications. Her debut book This Same Small Town in Each of Us, a collection of short memoir, poetry and flash fiction, released on October 30, 2011. She is currently compiling a second book consisting of primarily narrative poetry.

William Crawford is the author of *Fire in the Marrow (NeoPoiesis Press)*. His writing has been twice nominated for the Pushcart Prize. His work has been published globally in numerous magazines and anthologies. His second collection of poetry, *Actual Tigers*, shall be released in 2012. Currently, his poetry is being translated into Polish. William abides in Philadelphia, Pennsylvania, and is an animal rights activist.

Yair Ben-Zvi was born in Israel and raised in Los Angeles, is 25 years on the wander culling influence where he can find it and trying to make something work of the words he can put together. His English Degree from UCLA is only for show.

Zachary Guadamour now considers himself officially an Old Fuck. At one time he knew something about the law, but has worked at forgetting that. He considers himself fortunate he had the opportunity to study with Richard Shelton, Steve Orlen and Peter Wild, and with fellow students Alberto Rios, Peggy Shumaker, Iven Lourie, Michael Hogan and others. His first love has always been anthropological linguistics and consequently he is organizing an expedition to the Sahara of memory in search of the archaeological remains of the first word ever spoken.

Chris Billings is the Assistant Chairman of the Sun Poet's Society and an administrator for the largest online poetry workshop on the planet, Open City 360 Poets and Writers on Facebook. Chris makes his home in Schertz, Texas.